THE Twelve
Days of Christmas

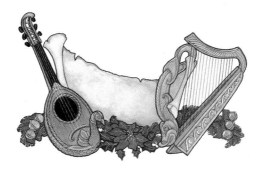

THE *Twelve*

For Lia

Illustrated by JAN BRETT

Days of Christmas

G. P. Putnam's Sons
New York

THE TWELVE DAYS

English traditional carol

VERSES 1-4

1. On the first* day of Christ-mas my
2. On the se-cond* day of Christ-mas my

true love gave to me a
true love gave to me

four col-ly birds, three French hens, two tur-tle-doves, and a par-tridge in a pear tree.
four three two

VERSES 5-12

5. On the fifth* day of Christ-mas my true love gave to me twelve lords a-leap-ing,
6. On the sixth* day of Christ-mas my true love gave to me twelve

*Sing appropriate number of day, and then cut from † to appropriate boxed number.

OF CHRISTMAS

e-lev'n la-dies danc-ing, ten pi-pers pi-ping,
e-lev'n ten

nine drum-mers drum-ming, eight maids a-milk-ing,
nine eight

sev'n swans a-swim-ming, six geese a-lay-ing, five gold rings, four col-ly birds,
sev'n six

three French hens, two tur-tle-doves, and a par-tridge in a pear tree.

n the first day of Christmas

My true love gave to me
A partridge in a pear tree.

On the second day of Christmas
My true love gave to me

Two turtledoves,
And a partridge in a pear tree.

Natalie

On the third day of Christmas
My true love gave to me
Three French hens,

Two turtledoves,
And a partridge in a pear tree.

On the fourth day of Christmas
My true love gave to me
Four colly birds,

Three French hens,
Two turtledoves,
And a partridge in a pear tree.

On the fifth day of Christmas
My true love gave to me
Five gold rings,
Four colly birds,

Three French hens,
Two turtledoves,
And a partridge in a pear tree.

© KERSTDAGEN

On the sixth day of Christmas
My true love gave to me
Six geese a-laying,
Five gold rings,

Four colly birds,
Three French hens,
Two turtledoves,
And a partridge in a pear tree.

На illustration banner: СЧАСТЛИВОГО

On the seventh day of Christmas
My true love gave to me
Seven swans a-swimming,
Six geese a-laying,
Five gold rings,

Four colly birds,
Three French hens,
Two turtledoves,
And a partridge in a pear tree.

РОЖДЕСТВА!

On the eighth day of Christmas
My true love gave to me
Eight maids a-milking,
Seven swans a-swimming,
Six geese a-laying,

Five gold rings,
Four colly birds,
Three French hens,
Two turtledoves,
And a partridge in a pear tree.

On the ninth day of Christmas
My true love gave to me
Nine drummers drumming,
Eight maids a-milking,
Seven swans a-swimming,
Six geese a-laying,

Five gold rings,
Four colly birds,
Three French hens,
Two turtledoves,
And a partridge in a pear tree.

On the tenth day of Christmas
My true love gave to me
Ten pipers piping,
Nine drummers drumming,
Eight maids a-milking,
Seven swans a-swimming,

Six geese a-laying,
Five gold rings,
Four colly birds,
Three French hens,
Two turtledoves,
And a partridge in a pear tree.

On the eleventh day of Christmas
My true love gave to me
Eleven ladies dancing,
Ten pipers piping,
Nine drummers drumming,
Eight maids a-milking,
Seven swans a-swimming,

Six geese a-laying,
Five gold rings,
Four colly birds,
Three French hens,
Two turtledoves,
And a partridge in a pear tree.

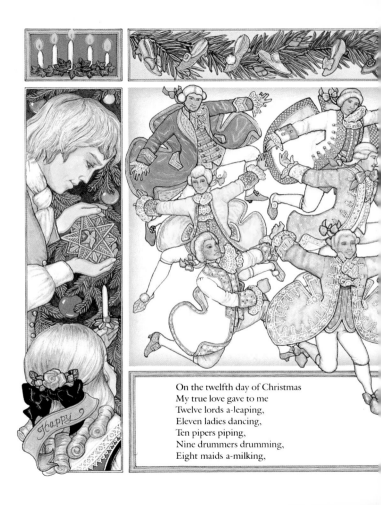

On the twelfth day of Christmas
My true love gave to me
Twelve lords a-leaping,
Eleven ladies dancing,
Ten pipers piping,
Nine drummers drumming,
Eight maids a-milking,

Seven swans a-swimming,
Six geese a-laying,
Five gold rings,
Four colly birds,
Three French hens,
Two turtledoves,
And a partridge in a pear tree.

G. P. Putnam's Sons, 200 Madison Avenue, New York, NY 10016
Originally published in 1986 by Dodd, Mead & Co., Inc.
Published simultaneously in Canada.
Printed in Singapore by Tien Wah Press (Pte) Ltd.
L.C. Number: 89-43065   ISBN 0-399-22197-2
1 3 5 7 9 10 8 6 4 2

Music adapted from *Carols for Christmas*, compiled and arranged by David Willcocks.
Copyright © 1983 by The Metropolitan Museum of Art. Reprinted by permission of
Henry Holt and Company, Inc.